Famous Butterfly Species
From Yellowtail to Viceroy

Science for Kids (Lepidopterology)

Children's Biological Science of Butterflies Books

PRODIGYWIZARD
BOOKS

Butterflies fascinate everyone. We cannot help smiling when we see their bright and vibrant colors and their graceful dance. Yes, butterflies are awesome!

Butterflies are day-flying insects. They are familiar to most humans for they are often seen in flowers. It is estimated that there are 17,500 butterfly species all over the world. Now, let's get to know some of the most beautiful and famous butterfly species.

Goliath Birdwing Butterfly
(Otnithoptera goliath)

This species is known to be the second-largest butterfly ever recorded. Its wings have yellow, black and green colors. It has a yellow and black body. This species is commonly found in Indonesia.

Karner Blue Butterfly
(Lycaeides Melissa samuelis)

Kamer Blue looks cute with its 1 inch wingspan. It lives in the pine barrens of the northern United States and in Ontario in Canada. The male and female of this species differ in appearance, but both of them have the same color scheme on the underside of their wings.

Monarch Butterfly
(Danaus plexippus)

This is a poisonous butterfly because they store a toxin called Cardiac Glycosides. In its larval stage it eats milkweed and at the same time lays eggs on it. It has a wingspan of 8.6-12.4 cm.

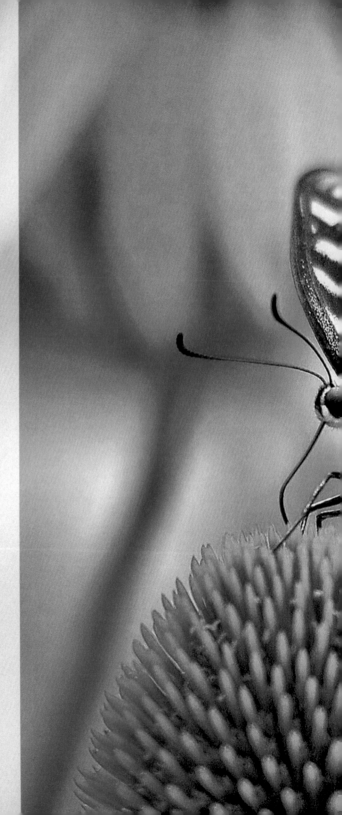

Tiger Swallowtail Butterfly
(Papilio glaucas)

It can be identified and seen easily because of its designs. Its wings and body have distinctive yellow and black striped patterns. It is found in the USA and Canada. Its caterpillar looks cute, for it is plump with yellow eye spots.

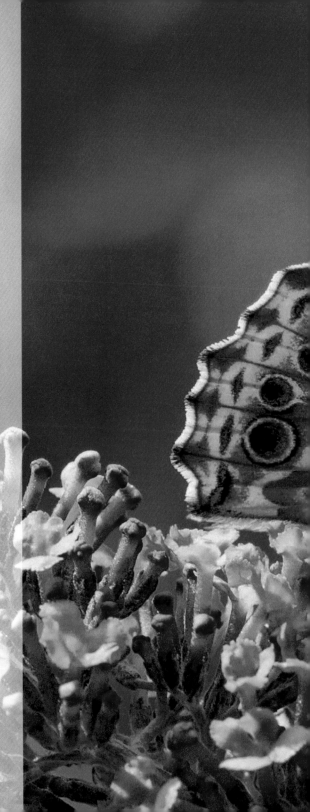

Painted Lady Butterfly
(Vanessa cardui)

This beauty is found in temperate and tropical areas. It is also known as the thistle butterfly, and has a wingspan of 5.1-7.3 cm. It belongs to the family Nymphalidae.

Zebra Swallowtail Butterfly
(Eurytides Marcellus)

The elongated tails on its back wings make this butterfly more adorable. It has distinctive black and white designs and a wingspan of 5-7cm. It belongs to the family Papilionidae. It lives in the eastern part of North America.

Peacock Butterfly
(Inachis oi)

This butterfly species is found in temperate parts of Europe and Asia. When it sees a bird, it rubs its wings together to produce a hissing sound. Its wings resemble to an owl's face. It belongs to the brush-footed butterflies family Nymphalidae.

Viceroy
(Limenitis archippus)

It has a resemblance to the Monarch butterfly. But it is smaller than a Monarch and has a black line that runs across its wings. It's a non-poisonous butterfly species with a wingspan of 7-7.5cm. It lives from Canada to Mexico.

Along with the moths, butterflies are part of an insect class in the order Lepidoptera. Whether the butterflies look bizarre, strange or unusual, they still appear remarkable because of their colourful wings. They are indeed very noticeable because of their graceful flight that shows off those wings. They are attracted to flowers. Planting flowering plants is a good idea so these pretty winged creatures visit our homes. What do you think?